ENDORS

Finding Value in a Cracked Pot gives a unique example of how God takes the broken pieces of our lives and makes something more valuable and more beautiful with them if we will only allow Him to do so.

—Kary Oberbrunner, Author of
Your Secret Name and *The Deeper Path*

Jan Henryson offers an authentic and vulnerable portrait of active faith through the trials of life. There is something for everyone in these pages—experiences of fear doubt, trauma, and ultimately, grace—in navigating the beauty and brokenness of existence. Brew a pot of tea, fine a comfortable chair, and curl up with this gentle testimony to the love and goodness of God.

—Rev. Dr. Travis D Else,
Executive Pastor of Preaching & Care,
First Reformed Church, Sioux Center, IA

In Jan Henryson's *Finding Value in a Cracked Pot,* the authors autobiography, I am reminded of what Ralph Waldo Emerson said, "In my walk, every man I meet is my superior in some way and in that I learn from him" in this case her. Jan is sincere recalling the seasons of cloud and sunshine in her life while looking to her faith for strength and as her true North Star. She expresses this in the apt but valuable metaphor of a cracked pot where she truly finds value from and through her trials. 1 Peter 1:7. *These have come so that the proven genuineness of your faith of greater worth than gold, which perishes even though refined by fire may result in praise, glory and honor when Jesus Christ is revealed.*

—Dr. Brian Johnson,
Orthopedic Surgeon, CNOS,
Dakota Dunes, SD

In *Finding Value in a Cracked Pot* Jan shows the readers through her life experiences, how God desires to not just restore her life, but also theirs. She gives a beautiful example of how God takes those broken pieces of our lives and makes something more valuable.

—Niccie Kliegl, CLC, RN,
Founder of Fulfill Your Legacy,
Author of *Awaking the Living Legacy*
and *Embracing the Loving Legacy*

I have known Jan Henryson for about 20 years from the early days of Center for Financial Education. Jan has persevered and carried out God's calling for her to start the CFE ministry. The passion and tender heart that Jan has for sharing Christ's love especially with those less fortunate is amazing. Jan proves that when you have a passion and dedicate yourself to something seeking God's direction, you can accomplish amazing things.

—Ron Heemstra, long-time friend
and former CFE board president

Teacher, mentor, advocate, director, and friend are just a few of the titles Jan Henryson has had over the years. I had the pleasure of working alongside her as the leader of a non-profit organization, helping individuals and families put the pieces of their financial puzzle together. Jan would see people often at their lowest and through friendship, prayer, and the unwillingness to give up, she helped them put the pieces together. Her commitment to seeing the best in others even when they couldn't see it themselves is an example we can all strive for. Our Father in Heaven has the same desire for each of his children to succeed. We don't always see how he will put the pieces together, but with the help of people like Jan and her willingness to share her heart, the world will be a more beautiful place.

Thanks for being you Jan!

—Aaron Haverdink, Financial Advisor,
former CFE board president

I'm excited about this book because the little lady that lived it is a life-long giver. Jan was a very successful 4th grade teacher for many years but felt the call to help those who struggled with their personal finances. So, she founded CFE and has done just that for over 20 years. We need more people just like Jan Henryson! Thanks for honoring me to do this.

—Dave Mulder, former teacher,
coach, State Senator, and CFE board member

No life journey is ordinary nor predictable as shared by Jan Henryson in her book, *Finding Value in a Cracked Pot*. Through her candid disclosure of her life's narrative, Jan teaches us that her struggles, misgivings and insecurities, or even the uncertainty in her faith are not uncommon, but a part of the human experience. With each chapter, she shares how God loves and sees her for who she is - with all her flaws and brokenness - and unfolds His plan for her as she learns throughout her life to seek His will in fulfilling His purpose for her. Jan's story inspires, encourages, and gives us hope that God - who loves us unconditionally - has a plan for us, too. To springboard us on our journey, Jan being a life-long learner—includes questions at the end of every chapter for self-reflection.

—Mary Zimmerman,
Iowa State University PTAC

FINDING VALUE IN A CRACKED POT

FAITH TO OVERCOME ✝ JOY IN FORGIVENESS
HOPE IN JESUS CHRIST

JAN HENRYSON

✝ AUTHOR
ACADEMY elite

Published by Author Academy Elite
P.O. Box 43, Powell, OH 43035
www.AuthorAcademyElite.com

Library of Congress Control Number: 2020906610

Paperback: 978-1-64746-231-4
Hardback: 978-1-64746-232-1
Ebook: 978-1-64746-233-8

Available in hardcover, softcover, and e-book.

Dedication

I want to dedicate this book to my amazing husband who has encouraged, supported, and journeyed with me through life and creating this book. Our daughter, Chris, has been instrumental with formatting this book and many other things. All our children and their spouses have encouraged and supported me from the beginning. Matt has been very influential in the designing of the cover. Ryan has shared many of his writing skills with me, and Kari has assisted with computer skills that I unfortunately lack. I am so grateful to each one. Many others have been instrumental in proofreading and beta reading this manuscript. Each of you has blessed me with your help and encouragement.

TABLE OF CONTENTS

FOREWORD

HOME STRONG HOME

For many generations, young children have loved to sing the action-packed Biblical chorus about the wise man who built his house on the rock. The falling rains and the rising floods threatened the security of that dwelling place—*but the house on the rock stood firm.* Yet the fun-filled climax for the singers came in the spirited action illustration of the next verse that depicted the calamity of the foolish man's ill-advised real estate selection. *The house on the sand fell flat!*

Another church song that also parallels the warning message of our Lord's closing parable of the Sermon on the Mount is recorded in Matthew 5-7. In the triumphant hymn, "The Solid Rock," we confidently sing a confession of faith, leaning wholly on Jesus' name, our solid rock. We proclaim our Savior's reliability through the deepest floodwaters of adversity.

It is this helpful motif of excellence in home construction that Jan Henryson enlists to portray a Biblically sound architecture for wise living. As a teacher, life coach, family member, and financial advisor, Henryson has often witnessed the vicissitudes of life that complicate daily living. The author's pilgrimage, coupled with knowledge gained as a life counselor, has been formative in developing solid values that Henryson now passes on to readers. Unfortunately, the building of that much-anticipated home is rarely without delays, obstacles, and disappointments. Henryson candidly shares with readers her days of gray skies and heavy rains. But founded on Scripture, buttressed by the strength of the Lord, and covered by abundant grace, the home of God's child is faithfully constructed so that it will stand firm.

Jan Henryson writes with authenticity and clarity. In her book, the reader will discover practical wisdom, hope, and humor. Her thoughtful applications of God's enduring Word will serve as an inspiring blueprint to those who seek to build their secure home of faith amidst the storms of life.

—Rev. Stephen C. Breen

PREFACE

Have you ever felt unworthy? Have you been afraid? Have you felt like your life was a failure? Have you felt unloved? I believe each one of us has experienced at least one of these emotions at one time or another. Life is hard!

However, the good news is there is hope! Hope can be found in a relationship with Jesus Christ. Now, before you close this book without giving it a chance, let me share.

We all have disappointments, losses, failures, and fear. But if we allow those feelings to control our lives, we miss so much. There is hope. We need to search for it and find that true hope that each of us can have. In *Finding Value in a Cracked Pot,* we see a struggle to overcome and find the freedom that is ours in Jesus.

Have you heard of the Japanese art of Kintsugi? Recently, I learned about this from a friend. For centuries, Japanese people have been fixing broken pottery with a special lacquer dusted with powdered gold, silver, or platinum. The beautiful seams glint in the cracks of the pottery and gives a unique look to each piece.

Imagine—this very technique can happen in our lives if we will only allow it to. Journey with me as I have been learning how God can use all the broken pieces of our lives for beauty.

THE FOUNDATION

Start children off on the way they should go, and even when they are old they will not turn from it.
—Proverbs 22:6

A sharp cry from the delivery room told the world I had arrived. My parents were overjoyed to have a little girl. They were very concerned, however, that I was only four pounds fourteen ounces. But the doctor told them I was healthy enough to go home with my mom because even though I was so tiny, I was a strong, feisty baby. (Little did they realize how feisty I was!) I am not so sure my mom was quite so happy a few days later because I heard the stories that I kept her up all night. The lack of sleep may have changed some of that joy to pure exhaustion, but they still felt blessed to have a little girl.

I heard I was a very fussy baby, and my mother wore out her chenille robe rocking me. I do not think this is accurate because my mom was *older*—according to medical standards —when I was born, and I believe she loved cuddling me, her precious bundle. Have you ever wondered what it would be like to grow up as an only child? Well, it is not as exciting as

1

most would expect. At least it wasn't for me. When you think about it, when something goes missing or breaks, there is no one to blame but the only child.

In my mind, at about five years old, I had a brilliant idea to invent an imaginary brother who I named Albert. Albert was amazing! He stole cookies for me and broke things, which, of course, I never would have done! This seemed like a perfect solution because in my way of thinking, my parents would never know I was the culprit. After several months of *Albert-behavior*, my dad came home on a lunch break and sat on Albert! I immediately began to cry unconsolably, and Mom and Dad could not understand why. Finally, I blurted out that Dad sat on Albert, and now Albert was dead. It was a tremendous tragedy.

My parents knew all along what I was doing, but I thought I was getting away with all of the pranks. At that point, they explained they knew about Albert, but they loved me so much—they knew eventually I would tell the truth.

Wow! That was a surprise to me. I had not realized how wise my parents really were. Through the years, I learned many more times that their wisdom was a true gift from God. I was very blessed to grow up where Christ was the head of my home. Mom and Dad took the time to teach me about God's Word and taught me to pray. Their love for me exemplified Christ's love for us. No, they were not perfect, but they lived what they believed.

They taught me that God loves me. He loved me so much that He sent His son, Jesus, to die on the cross to pay for the naughty things I had done, even the pranks I blamed on *Albert*. Although I did not fully comprehend this, I knew deep down that I wanted Jesus to live in my life. So, at a very young age, I asked Jesus to come into my heart. But I still believed that for my parents and God to really love me, I had to be a good, even *perfect* daughter.

Our first home was a little house by the railroad tracks. When the trains came by in the afternoon, Mom and I went outside and waved at the conductors. The conductors responded by tooting the horn and throwing a piece of candy or a penny to me. That was very exciting as a little girl. I thought of them as my friends and could not wait until the next day to see them.

There were several other girls in the neighborhood, and we built tents out of blankets on the clotheslines, built castles in the sand box, played with our dolls, and had so much fun. In the summer, we swam in wash tubs and ran through the water from sprinklers.

When I was about five years old, my parents built a new house a few blocks from where we lived. My uncle and dad designed and built much of the home themselves. My parents worked extremely hard to make this not just a house, but a home. Finally, I had my own room. The first night in our new home, I caused a bit of excitement. I rolled out of my new bed onto the floor. It must have made quite a bang because Dad ran in to find me still asleep on the floor under the bed.

New friends and adventures came with the new house. Now there were roller skates, bicycles, and forts in the dirt hills next door where the construction of another home was happening. There was never a lack of something to do. During this time, one of my friends from my old neighborhood, Janice, came over to my new house a lot. Our favorite thing was to play school. As I remember, I always wanted to be the teacher, and she never objected. We both loved drawing and writing on my large blackboard my mother's brother, Rein, made for me. He was an excellent carpenter and built many other pieces of furniture and toys that I still treasure.

One night, Janice slept in a tent in her backyard with one of her siblings. A rabid skunk crawled into their tent. She became very ill and was in the hospital for many weeks. Sadly, she never recovered. It was my first real experience with death. Then, I was afraid to go to sleep at night because my young mind did not really comprehend what had happened to her. I asked my parents a lot of questions like, "Where did Janice go? How do you know that she is in heaven? Where is heaven?", among other questions. It was difficult for my parents to explain death to a little one. I looked at Janice *sleeping* so peacefully in this wooden box and could not understand why she would not wake up. Death is a very difficult concept for an adult and even more so to a small child.

Facing death as a child was really the beginning of recognizing brokenness in my life. Yes, there were many broken pieces before this—little lies, stealing cookies, not listening—and many more pieces that encompass a child, but death was suddenly a reality. Is there a way to fix this? The only way is through faith in the promises we have that if we believe in Christ and accept Him as our Savior and Lord, then we will be with Him after we die. It is a promise, and God's promises are unbreakable. Many years later, I can see those broken pieces now reformed and reshaped as He continues to lead and guide my life.

CHAPTER 1 THOUGHTS

What was your early childhood like?

_____

_____

_____

_____

What was your relationship with your siblings?

_____

_____

_____

_____

Do you remember your first encounter with the death of someone close to you? How did you react? What were some of your thoughts?

_____

_____

_____

_____

What effect did this loss have on you?

_____

_____

_____

_____

How did this loss make you feel?

_____

_____

_____

_____

What broken pieces of your life do you struggle with?

_____

_____

_____

_____

PILLARS

Children are a gift from Him, offspring are a reward from Him.
—Psalm 127:3

One of my earliest memories is of my grandmother Handeland. She was my mother's mother. She and Grandpa came to America from Norway as a young couple with several young children in tow. I cannot imagine an ocean voyage with several small children, but with courage and God's grace, they made that trip to Iowa. They promised they would return to Norway to their families in three years, but that never happened. Once settled here in the United States, they had several more children. My mother was the second youngest of eleven siblings. Before my mother was born, Grandpa and Grandma's oldest son drowned in the Des Moines River. He was only fourteen at the time, and it was very difficult for my grandparents. I recently located newspaper articles of his drowning and was able to learn details of that tragic day. Now I understand my grandparent's confusion with a new country compounded by the unfathomable grief over losing a child.

I was the youngest of the grandchildren, but I had the privilege of spending time with my grandma. She sat in her rocking chair with her Bible opened on her lap rocking back and forth, mumbling—or so I assumed that is what her words were. Courageously, I asked my aunt what she was doing. "Grandma is praying in Norwegian for her children, grandchildren, great-grandchildren, their spouses, and so on." Her prayers carried through the generations with answers in ways she could not begin to know or understand. She was truly a Godly woman who believed deeply in the power of prayer. As our children have grown and our grandchildren have blessed our lives, the answers to her prayers and others' prayers is evident. At the time, I had no concept of what those prayers could do and how they would impact many lives. My grandfather passed away before I was born, and Grandma's English was somewhat limited. I am sure she felt very alone because she was only able to speak fluently with her immediate family. Yet God heard her prayers. He understands all languages, especially the language of prayer.

One of my grandmother's rules was never to use scissors on Sunday, or something bad would happen. (Why that was important I never knew, but it was the rule.) One Sunday, I grabbed scissors out of the kitchen drawer, took my paper doll book, and scooted under the kitchen table. Yes, Grandma was correct. Something bad did happen. I made a V-shaped cut in the very front skirt of the red taffeta my aunt had just finished making for me. I don't remember much of what happened next except I never used scissors on Sunday again until I was an adult. My aunt cried because I ruined the dress she spent hours making, even hand sewing the lace on it.

In our new home, we had so much more room to entertain. Often, my parents had friends or family over for a meal or coffee. We even got a parakeet (we learned much later that I was allergic to feathers) that we had a great time teaching to talk. However, one time he was inappropriate. My parents invited our new pastor and his wife over for Sunday dinner. Dad began to pray a blessing over our food when the parakeet very loudly shouted, "Shut up!" followed by "Pretty Dickie," which was the bird's name. Was I ever in trouble! The pastor and his wife had a good laugh, and I had a good talking to later!

It was especially fun on Sunday afternoons to spend time with my cousins. Many of them lived very close to us, within about fifteen miles, so we gathered for Sunday dinners or afternoon coffee. Sometimes we gathered at one of my grandparents' homes. My grandpa and grandma Espeset, my dad's parents, also lived very close to our home. We filled the time with games, croquet, and softball. In the wintertime, we did jigsaw puzzles or board games. It was special because as an only child, I did not have the normal brother and sister experience. So, this was special and a learning experience because we argued and quarreled, but in the end, we laughed a lot and had fun.

Fishing and camping were special for us because we lived very close to the Iowa Great Lakes. My uncles and aunts loved to fish as well. I have a very vivid memory of one beautiful summer day when my uncle Rein bought a new station wagon. It was a blue and white vehicle, and he was pretty proud of that purchase! I thought it was beautiful and felt very special when he took me for rides in it, usually followed by an ice cream stop. That was really fun!

On that summer day, Uncle Rein decided to go fishing one afternoon by himself. He parked his new wagon on the hill and walked down to the shore line to begin casting. He heard a noise. All of a sudden, the station wagon came careening down the hill right into the lake. Now he was in a pickle. He was alone. There were no cell phones, and he was several miles from the nearest phone. He never shared how he got help, but the station wagon was unrecognizable when it was later pulled out of the lake. We never talked about it when he was around, but I know there were several laughs about his *biggest catch.*

Through this time, prayer and the Bible were the most important elements of each day. Mealtimes always began with prayer. We started the evening meal with a scripture passage or devotional. God was the glue that held the family together in good times and in bad. I am so thankful for parents who taught me God's word, prayed with me, and helped me understand the tremendous sacrifice Christ made for me. In fact, the first table prayer I learned was in Norwegian, and I remember it to this day. Even in the most difficult times, my parents' faith sustained them and caused them to grow even closer to their Heavenly Father.

At Easter time, my Grandmother Espeset made the cutest little nests for each place setting at the table. There were three jelly beans in each nest. Grandma cooked by memory. She never used a physical recipe card, so the recipe for the nests or her famous banana cake with chocolate icing are hard to imitate. Many of us tried to recreate them but none tastes like Grandma's.

At that time, we walked to school, which worked out great for me because Grandma Handeland's house was on my way home. I stopped at her house almost every afternoon, and I was not the only regular guest. A cousin who lived about two blocks from her house had a cocker spaniel named Skipper. Skipper seemed to know when I stopped there. So, we met there and usually received a delicious sugar cookie from one of the big tins in the kitchen. They were always filled with cookies, sugar, raisins, and a variety of other flavors depending on the week. Skipper and I were great friends! When my grandmother passed away, my aunt thought I should have the tin. It was a toss-up between Skipper and me, but he didn't have hands! I treasure the tin to this day and the memories of such good times.

Christmas was filled with goodies, especially lutefisk and lefse. Lutefisk originally was cod fish soaked in lye to preserve it. Today it is not soaked in lye, but you still need to let it soak in salt water briefly before it is cooked. Lefse is made of potatoes and flour, rolled very thin, and cooked on a griddle while basted with milk. Ah! Oh, how delicious that feast was. We opened presents on Christmas Eve after the dishes were done. But probably my most precious memory is when we gathered around Grandma's pump organ singing Christmas carols. Mom's family was very musical, and the beauty of the carols in four-part harmony and the memory of those times still brings me tears of joy every Christmas. It was truly a sacred moment that I will always treasure.

Childhood was pretty normal until the summer I was about ten years old. My mom returned to work about that time, so I spent quite a bit of time alone or over at my aunt's house. During a beautiful summer day, a man my parents knew came by our house. He asked about my parents but when I told him they were not home, he came in the house anyway. We sat down and talked, but he began doing things I did not understand and did not like. He fondled me inappropriately, gave me a kiss on the cheek when he left, and told me this was our little secret. Since I wanted to be a good daughter, I kept it a secret.

As time went on, he returned a number of times. I tried to hide but somehow, he always found me. Finally, I locked all the doors of the house when I was alone. My parents never understood why. They thought I was being a little skittish.

These incidents in my past really helped me to understand why women do not disclose abuse. It is very embarrassing. I blamed myself for many years. To this day, I cannot imagine telling my parents, not so much because they would not have believed me, but describing what had happened would have been so degrading. I often wonder how they would have handled the situation, but I will never know.

Much later, I learned the term for this is abuse, and it affected my life in many ways. It became very difficult to really trust anyone, even my Heavenly Father. These were huge broken pieces, and God is still putting them back together in my life.

In high school, my goal was to strive for perfection. I believed I was never good enough. There were many activities I participated in besides classes—band, choir, and speech, among others. When I came home with a report card of all A's, except for deportment, which was a B, my parents' only comment was, "Why did you receive a B in deportment?" I explained that no one was perfect, and B was the highest grade. My parents did not mean to send the message that B was not good enough, but in my mind, it was another reminder that I was not good enough. I graduated second in my class out of two hundred, and I still had regrets. What could I have done differently to have finished first? I was still looking for unachievable perfection. What would make me good enough?

One of my school teachers was also my Sunday school teacher during my senior year. As I left the room after taking the physics semester test, I remarked, "I hope you have as much *fun* correcting this as I had taking it." It was a very sarcastic remark. When I walked into our Sunday school class a few days later, the teacher looked at me and said, "I had a great time correcting your test. You had the highest score in the class." It was hard for me to believe until I saw the paper. I stayed in touch with this teacher. My husband and I visit this teacher when I am in my home town, and even with all the students he has had, he never forgot that experience. And I know I never will.

During that time, I heard in church, Sunday school, and catechism that God loved me because I was His child. Those words were only words. I heard them but did not believe it applied to me because I thought I needed to do things perfectly. Of course, that was not possible. God's grace was a topic I learned about, studied, and repeated, but I always felt I needed to strive to be perfect.

CHAPTER 2 THOUGHTS

What are some of your favorite childhood memories?

_____

_____

_____

_____

How have your memories influenced your life?

_____

_____

_____

_____

When did you first learn about Christ?

_____

_____

_____

_____

Who or what had the greatest influence on you when you were growing up?

_____

_____

_____

_____

What broken pieces did this chapter bring to mind?

_____

_____

_____

_____

UTILITIES

Praise Him with the sounding of the trumpet, praise him with the harp and lyre, praise Him with timbrel and dancing, praise Him with the strings and pipe, praise Him with the clash of cymbals, praise Him with resounding cymbals.
—Psalm 150:3-5

Music was a part of my life almost from the beginning. Mom sang "Jesus Loves Me" and many other choruses as I grew up. My aunt, uncle, mom, and a family friend sang in a quartet. I loved the rich harmony from each piece they sang. It was the same at holidays when our extended family was together. Music was a part of most of those gatherings. Usually a meal began with singing a table prayer.

One Wednesday evening in Lent, the quartet was to sing for the Lenten service at our church. For some reason, I was jumping on my parent's bed (which was never allowed), and I fell back and hit my head on the dresser. Off we went to the emergency room for stitches. While the cover was over my head during the stitches, my dad promised me chicks for Easter that I had been begging for.

We went to the store and picked out three beautifully spotted chicks. Mom and I did not know what we were about to experience. Dad made a pen in the basement and then lined it with newspaper. The newspapers had to be changed often, and the chicks needed food and water frequently. As the chicks grew, their spots disappeared. They grew quickly, and it reached the point where their crowing became very annoying. Dad arranged with a farming friend to take the chickens to his place. Much later, I learned that the neighbor's dog caught up with my chicks. It was a sad day.

At the age of five, I began to take piano lessons. As I practiced, my parakeet often sat on my shoulder and chirped along. My first recital was memorable. I had my pretty dress with my cloth handkerchief in my hand. As I got up to play my piece, "The Waltzing Parakeet," I did not know what to do with the handkerchief. I decided to hold it in my left hand while I played. It definitely was not a waltzing parakeet. It was more like a thudding one. I will never forget the shocked look in mom's eyes when I sat down. There were several chuckles in the audience as well.

Lessons continued with different teachers and much practicing. I also began taking organ lessons. My cousin asked me to play for her wedding when I was only fourteen years old. I was extremely nervous and practiced many hours for that event. Everything went smoothly, and my cousin was very pleased.

In high school, I started to give piano lessons, which continued through my college years and into the early years in my marriage. It has been a joy to see some of my students really use the talent God has given them to glorify Him. I like to think I had a little part in that, but God is the one who gave them the joy and encouragement to continue.

Taking organ lessons in college was intimidating. I heard the professors play and wondered how I would ever measure up. I never reached their levels of proficiency, but I learned much from these musicians.

When I got my first apartment, I saved for two years and finally had the resources to purchase a piano. I cannot express the joy I felt as that instrument was delivered to my apartment. I am not sure my neighbors enjoyed it, but I never received any complaints.

Music has been my outlet as frustrations have arisen, a comfort when I have lost a loved one, an expression of joy. But most of all, it has been one of the biggest blessings and my way of worship.

Unfortunately, after the car accident I had on my way to practice at church, I had to have numerous shoulder surgeries. It became very clear that even after therapy, I would not be playing the organ again except occasionally for my enjoyment. That was an enormous loss for me because it was my way to express my praise, hurts, and prayers. It took a long time to really accept that as my new reality, but I came to appreciate listening to others so skillfully make the organ sing. I admit for several years I asked God *why*. I know God has a plan much better than mine, and I may never learn why in my lifetime.

Often God allows us to go through storms so we can grow closer to Him. He is with us through the storms, and if we focus on Him, we can remain in the eye of the storm where it is calm. Because He is in control, we can remain calm for He loves us and has a plan for us. His plan for me is far different than the ones I have had for my life, but without a doubt, I can trust that His plan is best.

One of the joys of my life is listening to my grandchildren sing. It is so special to see that my love of music has been passed to them.

CHAPTER 3 THOUGHTS

What are some things in your life you really enjoyed doing?

_____

_____

_____

_____

Has anything interfered with your plans or dreams? If so, what?

_____

_____

_____

_____

What storms have you encountered in your life?

_____

_____

_____

_____

Have you leaned into God in these storms? If so, what have you learned?

_____

_____

_____

_____

If you did not lean on God, what occurred?

_____

_____

_____

_____

Are you willing to let God lead you in his plan for your life?

_____

_____

_____

_____

Are you beginning to see God transforming the broken pieces
of your life into something better?

_____

_____

_____

_____

PORTALS

I have the strength to face all conditions by the power that
Christ gives me.
—Philippians 4:13

My earliest memories involve playing school. My uncle even built a combination, six-foot-tall blackboard and bulletin board. The dolls were my students, and some were very challenging. My neighborhood friends came over to our basement, and we played school for hours on end when the weather was not nice enough to be outside. I loved it. I knew I wanted to be a teacher.

As I began college, I knew what my major would be—Elementary Education. Most of my friends were struggling to figure out what they wanted to do, but my decision never wavered. My dad had definite ideas of where I should spend my college years, but after visiting that school, I knew it was not a fit for me. I attended a graduation with my cousin, Mary Jo, at Augustana College in Sioux Falls, South Dakota, and it felt like the right place. Sioux Falls is a city about one hundred miles from Estherville, Iowa, the town in which I grew up. We spent a great deal of time as a family seeking God's direction, and it was clear Augustana College was the right choice. I majored in Elementary Education with minors in music and math.

As I continued my education at Augustana, my classes were okay, but my relationships with Christian friends were the best, and they were instrumental in my growth in my faith.

Student teaching was interesting. Because there were so many elementary education majors, we had to team teach. This meant I student-taught with another classmate. My partner and I were assigned to a new school, and we were the fourth pair of student teachers the class had that year. Plus, it was the fourth quarter of the school, which made it very difficult. These children were from a very exclusive neighborhood, had traveled the world on vacations to exotic places, and generally had no interest in learning. It was difficult to motivate them. My creative side had to engage in more ways to stimulate discussions and learning with this group. That push within myself helped me to develop a can-do attitude that I could face any challenge set before me.

There was a glut of education majors. It was challenging to find a position. I sent out many inquiries and résumés and then prayed and waited. I interviewed with a number of school districts, but none of them seemed right. One morning as I student taught, the principal's office called me for a phone call. The call was from a superintendent in a town called Sioux Center, Iowa. When he asked me to come for an interview, I did not even think before I responded, "Sure, I would like to come. Where is Sioux Center?" Sioux Center is a small town in the very Northwest corner of Iowa. While my response was not perfect, the interview with the principal was enough to convince me I had found a place where I could fit. I loved that they even opened each day in each classroom with devotions and prayer.

I prayed about this for several days until the phone call came offering me the job. Excited and scared, I moved to a town where I knew no one. Up until this time, I had always been in a situation where I knew someone. But there, I felt totally alone. God was graciously there with me each step of the way.

At the very first faculty meeting, they introduced the new teachers. On my turn, the superintendent announced, "We now have an integrated staff. We hired a Norwegian." I wondered what I had gotten myself into. As I looked over my class list, I understood. All the last names of the students were completely unfamiliar to me. I had landed in a Dutch community!

My class was challenging. I have to admit that some of the methods I used probably would not be acceptable today, but they worked. For example, when my students tried to make spit wads in class, their punishment was staying in for recess and making one hundred spit wads without getting a drink of water. If they were not able to complete the task during recess, they had to come in at the next recess and start all over. Obviously, it was not much fun for them. This class passed the message on to the next year, "Don't make spit wads in her class!" They had gotten the point. For the rest of my years of teaching, I never saw another spit wad in my classroom.

Dutch children grow tall. As our class walked down to the lunchroom for our meal, the principal came out of his office and exclaimed, "Where is your teacher?" I waved my hand at him, and the children chuckled. I realized fourth graders in this town were basically about my height, 5-feet 2-inches.

One day, one of my students was particularly difficult. He had not listened. He pestered other classmates, and he goofed off. I tried to ignore the behavior because that usually worked with him, but that day it did not. Finally, I told him very firmly to sit at his desk. The desk had a liftable lid with the contents inside. This student took me literally. He sat in his desk, and because he was too big for it, he got stuck. I know today's standards would not allow this, but at the time, I let him remain there until recess. The janitor assisted me in removing him from the desk. A number of years later, my husband and I had dinner in a neighboring town. This boy's mother walked in with her new husband. (The boy's father had died of cancer when he was in the upper grades.) She walked over to me and asked, "Do you remember me?" I knew who she was, but I was uncertain how I should respond. But I said yes as my heart pounded in my chest. I was afraid she would chastise me for what had happened in my classroom. Imagine my surprise when she said, "Do you remember my son getting stuck in his desk?"

"Yes," I answered with much trepidation.

She replied, "That was the best lesson he learned in elementary school." She went on to share that he had gone on to finish college and had a very successful career and family. She thanked me for helping him learn respect. Sometimes you never know how your actions or words will affect someone.

There was another boy who also would not listen. Finally, I took him out in the hall and explained that he needed to go to the principal's office. The student got on his hands and knees and begged me not to take him there. In those years, principals still were allowed to administer spankings. After thinking it over, I explained he had the option of entering back into the classroom, but if he did, his behavior had to be very good. That decision must have helped because that young man became an outstanding superintendent of schools when he grew up.

New faces appeared in my classroom every year. It was an adventure to discover how each one learned, and then I did my best to help them achieve the skills they would need for the next year. I wish I could say I always succeeded, but I did my very best and prayed for and cared for every student while they were *under my wings* and after.

Teaching is a difficult and challenging profession, even much more so today than when I taught. But children remain much the same. They each carry a story full of happiness *and* sadness. Because I saw them as God's dearly loved children, those years were a joy.

Every year, it was so difficult to say good bye to those wonderful lives I was blessed to be part of, but the promise of a new group of students the next year was encouraging. Each student came into my class wanting to be accepted, respected, and loved. Regardless of where or when children enter the classroom, when these expectations are met, children learn and their lives are forever changed.

I loved teaching. How refreshing to hear from former students that my class was so much fun because we laughed so much. Learning is fun, and when children understand that concept, they will work hard and accomplish many things. The fourth graders from my teaching years went on to do amazing things in life. I feel so fortunate I was able to share a tiny bit in their learning experience. Again, God put pieces of my life into the place where He wanted them to be.

CHAPTER 4 THOUGHTS

Did you have any specific dreams or ideas for after high school? If so, what were they?

_____

_____

_____

_____

Did your dreams happen, or did you change course? If so, why?

_____

_____

_____

What influenced the choices you made?

_____

_____

_____

_____

Are you happy with where you are currently? Why or why not?

_____

_____

_____

_____

What pieces do you see God putting back together in your life?

_____

_____

_____

_____

WINDOWS

Love is patient, love is kind. It does not envy. It does not boast.
It is not proud, it is not rude, it is not self-seeking, it is not
easily angered, it keeps no record of wrongs.
—1 Corinthians 13:4-7

College challenged me in so many ways. I was quiet, more of an introvert, but the newfound freedom of college changed that. There were great times with friends, late evening talks, and most importantly, a deepening of my faith and dependence on God. For the first time, I realized I was responsible for my choices and that those choices affected others. I empathized when others struggled with whatever life threw at them, and my heart broke for them. My best friend's father passed away during our junior year, and I was again confronted with our mortality. I leaned on my Heavenly Father and prayed and cried with my friend, which taught me so much about God's amazing grace and love for us. He blesses us even in our darkest times.

Those years also had a special meaning for me because I met a very special young man. Now, I have to admit that our first meeting was not exemplary! He happened to be my cousin's best friend, and to this day, when he and my cousin are together, they are very ornery! After I met Bruce, I made the comment to my cousin. "I sure hope you have nicer friends than Bruce!" Have you ever had to eat your words? I did, and they did not taste very good.

Bruce attended South Dakota State at Brookings. Brookings is only sixty miles from Sioux Falls where I attended school. I definitely believe God has a sense of humor since one of my good friends at college was Bruce's cousin, Bev. Since he was no longer under my cousin's influence, we discovered our common faith in Christ. Our children refer to that time as the dark ages because we did not have computers or cell phones. Instead, we sent letters and called each other, often late at night because that was when we were both free. These phone calls and letters continued when I moved to Sioux Center to teach. We were able to see each other fairly often but not as much as we would have liked. Bruce changed his major in college, so he spent an extra year in school. That meant he was still in close vicinity. I could hardly wait to get home from teaching to see if a letter awaited me. On Valentine's Day before we were engaged, I came home from school to find Bruce in my apartment with beautiful flowers in his hands. I am thankful we needed to communicate through letters because I believe that really strengthened our relationship.

As I got to know Bruce, I learned he was a very Godly young man. He was a man of faith, knew his Bible, and had a gift when it came to sharing his faith, and the power of his prayers were amazing. I began to learn about God's grace, which is totally undeserved. His love is amazing because He loves us just as we are. He created us. As Bruce and I grew closer, I started to realize who I was in Christ. I no longer had to strive for perfection—something I could never attain— because I was the person my Father created me to be.

In Jeremiah 29:11 we read, *"I know the plans I have for you, says the Lord. Plans to give you a future and a hope."* And God certainly knew the plan he had for us. A couple of years later, Bruce asked me to marry him. If I had continued to seek perfection in my life, I would have missed the opportunity of a lifetime and never had the privilege of sharing my life with him. It was through his love and acceptance that I started to believe God's Word was really true in my life. I had no problem accepting its truth for others, but for me, it was different. God's love came alive for the first time, and I began to understand that there was nothing I could do to make my Father love me more, and nothing I did would make Him love me less. His love is unconditional. What a great love that still amazes me each day!

God's plans are so much better than anything we could ask or think. He knew what I needed—Him! I needed to receive His unconditional love and grace before I could really love someone else the way I should.

After about two years of a long-distance relationship, Bruce proposed. He did not want an answer right away. He wanted me to think and pray about it for a week. (This was after I had been praying for quite some time that he would ask!)

We wanted our wedding to be Christ-centered. The scripture we chose is at the beginning of this chapter—1 Corinthians 13:4-7. Music is a very important part of my life, so we even hand-picked the prelude and postlude. We prayed for people to see Christ and His love through that service.

Our wedding day in June started off hot and sticky. There was not a cloud in the sky until about three hours before the wedding when the tornado sirens sounded. My parents and I were just getting ready to leave for the church when Mom insisted we go to the basement. As my feet touched the floor of the basement, I realized my wedding dress was upstairs. I begged and pleaded, but she would not let me go retrieve the dress.

The good news is the house was fine and so was my dress. The bad news is that many of our friends and neighbors did not share that good news. The tornado destroyed buildings, downed trees, and farmers lost many crops. Bruce was standing outside the hotel where he had stayed the previous night. One of the guests he invited to our wedding was a 93-year-old pastor who had played a big role in Bruce's faith walk. As they stood outside watching the storm, the pastor remarked, "That's the darkest cloud I've seen in all my ninety-three years!" Wow!

The rain stopped for guests to come into the church and then it lightninged, thundered, and poured throughout the ceremony. At the conclusion, my pastor loudly proclaimed, "That was the most inspiring funeral I have ever officiated at!" Imagine the look of horror on my face and the simultaneous laughter from Bruce over that comment. All of a sudden, the pastor got very red in the face and said, "I didn't just say what I think I said, did I?" I assured him he had and that it would be a long time, if ever, before I would forget about it.

We should have realized that foreshadowed the beginning of our life together and the storms of life we would face.

CHAPTER 5 THOUGHTS

Have your plans changed from what you thought your life would be when you were a child? What changes have you experienced?

_____

_____

_____

_____

Were you satisfied with the choices you made? Why or why not?

_____

_____

_____

What was the greatest influence on your choices?

_____

_____

_____

_____

How did you decide who to marry, or did you choose to remain single?

_____

_____

_____

_____

Did you invite God to be the center of your decisions? If God was not there, what would you have done differently? If God was present, how do you see his work in your life?

_____

_____

_____

_____

Again, do you see pieces of your life being put back together? What pieces still need mending?

_____

_____

_____

_____

BLUEPRINT

Know therefore that the Lord God, the faithful God who keeps covenant and steadfast love with those who love him and keep His commandments, to a thousand generations.
—Deuteronomy 7:9

Marriage is beautiful, but it is an adjustment. I had been teaching and living alone for three years when we got married. I had my way of doing things, and it was very comfortable to me. Bruce had also been living alone and was used to doing things his way. We both had a lot to learn about give and take. It was a challenging time but one I would never regret. One day, he walked in as I ironed the sheets for our bed. He asked, "What are you doing? We're just going to sleep on them so why do they need to be ironed?" Good question. My mom always ironed sheets, so I did too. Since then, I found he was pretty much right about the sheets. After one night, they are wrinkled anyway. I call that adapting!

I handled money meticulously. I budgeted to the penny. Our first actual quarrel came over the silliest purchase. Bruce went into town and bought four red plastic glasses for our home for one dollar. My mouth dropped open when he walked in. "What is that? It wasn't in the budget!" Money fights are very common to newlyweds, and we were no exception. Since then, we have learned to work together on our finances, and both of us have grown from the experience.

The summer we married, we managed Bruce's parents' KOA Campground. I found out that my husband was an excellent people person, very charismatic, able to talk with anyone, and could easily relate to them in a meaningful way. He could solve and resolve any problems that arose with the campers.

In the fall, we went back to Sioux Center where I was teaching, and Bruce began work at the local hospital. We were in a routine of work, church, and developing friendships. That fall, six doctors explained we would never be able to have any children. We were both devastated. We loved children and desperately wanted our own. I was angry with God, and I told Him so. We wanted to give a child a home, and we were a loving couple. When we were denied that possibility, I cried out to God. I begged Him to give us a child. After many months, we learned I was pregnant. But I miscarried and lost that joyful hope. Much later in my life, I realized I never gave myself the opportunity to really grieve for that child. Several years after that happened, I had a dream, and it became clear in my mind that the baby was a girl named Jennifer Lynn. I cannot explain how this happened, but I knew she was in heaven and loved by those who had gone before us. I knew we would see her one day. God's promises are so precious at times like that.

Heartbroken, I wondered if I could be the wife Bruce wanted if I could not give him any children. When I saw a baby in someone else's arms, I cried and asked *why* so often. As I began to work through my pain, I also started to see God's grace and His love for me. He loved me just as I was—His child. He loved me with all my flaws and brokenness. After all, He had made me perfectly imperfect. His love did not depend on anything I did or did not do. It was constant, accepting, and forgiving. I began to yield my will to His. It was not easy, but it was so worth it. My worth is in Him, because He made me exactly the way He wanted and needed me to be. He had a plan for me even before time began. Once again, my Father had my broken pieces to use to make me whole.

Several months later, we learned I was pregnant again. This time we were blessed with a tiny girl we named Christina Joy. Before she was born, we struggled over names. I wanted to spell her name with a *K,* but Bruce wanted to spell it with a *C.* After thirty hours of labor, our doctor asked, "How do you want to spell her name?"

My response was, "I really don't care!" I was exhausted, so *C* it was.

A few weeks later, we went to see Bruce's grandmother and introduced her to her new great-granddaughter. She looked at us and said, "It was so nice of you to name your daughter after me, but why did you spell it with a C instead of a K?"

I poked Bruce and said, "That question is for you." We did not know that Grandma's middle name was Kristina. We have had many laughs over that incident.

Chris, as we call her, was a lot of fun, and she was definitely a daddy's girl. I was still teaching at the time, and as I graded papers at night, the two of them snuggled up on the couch and took a nap. We felt so blessed to have this special little one in our lives and tried to enjoy every minute we could with her.

About two years later, we welcomed Matthew into our family. I realized the doctors do not always have the answers— God does, and His plan for our family to grow was definitely obvious.

Matthew was a challenge. He cried for twenty-three out of twenty-four hours. He turned blue and had a number of hospitalizations while doctors tried to determine what was wrong. He was not growing as he should.

We received many different diagnoses. He had a tumor somewhere, cystic fibrosis, an incurable heart disease, and many more. The doctors let us believe them for a few days or months, but then they came back to tell us that they were wrong, every time. They did not know what the problem was.

Finally, we took Matt to National Jewish Hospital in Denver, Colorado, where we finally received accurate answers. Matt was allergic to corn and corn products. Corn, in some form, is in many foods and also in infant formulas. But for me, the most meaningful part of that journey was the commute we made each day from where we stayed to the hospital where Matt was. The mountains were in front of us each morning, which reminded me of Psalm 121:1, *"I will lift my eyes to the hills. Where does my help come from? My help is in the name of the Lord."*

Because of Matt's many hospitalizations, I had to give up my teaching position, which was a difficult decision on many levels. I loved teaching and knew it would be a financial burden for our family. But who would be able to care for all the situations Matt faced? I became a stay-at-home Mom. As we look back, we saw how God provided in every situation. We always had food on the table and were able to pay our mortgage and other bills. Seeing God's provision gave us the opportunity to grow in our faith and to love and serve Him more. Again, God used our broken pieces to our benefit by His provision.

Four years later, baby Ryan was born. Ryan was a fun baby, full of smiles and giggles. Both Chris and Matt loved that this little guy joined our family. We truly felt blessed as a family, but I quickly learned about sibling fights. I could not imagine why my children were fighting with each other. I wondered why they could not be happy to have each other to play with. Bruce finally sat me down and assured me—an only child—that this was normal. I really had a lot to learn!

Two years later, we were blessed with our last little one, Kari. When Bruce came home to tell the other children they had a new baby sister, Ryan loudly cried, "But I wanted a puppy!" To this day, he still shares those sentiments from time to time. But Kari truly completed our family. *"Children are a heritage from the Lord"* (Psalm 127:3).

Four children were an adventure for me, an only child. Our children were really normal kids, but so many things surprised me. One day, I asked Chris to watch Matt while I ran downstairs to change the laundry. As I walked into the kitchen, I saw Matt pouring sugar from the canister onto the kitchen table. I looked at Chris, astounded. "I thought I asked you to watch your brother."

With complete innocence, she looked at me and said, "I am Mommy. I am." I learned that my instructions had to be clear and spelled out!

While they were growing up, we faced many challenges, but we always knew God was faithful and would see us through. I started to give piano lessons at home and really enjoyed that experience. During one lesson, Chris came to get me. She was very upset. I learned that Kari had climbed up the drawers in the kitchen, stood up on the counter, and found the *childproof* bottle of Benadryl. I ended all lessons that day and took Kari to the hospital where she was forced to drink activated charcoal. Despite the struggle, the nurses won. It was a long time before she took Benadryl after that and when she did, it was in pill form.

Matt was truly the artist in the family, and that talent definitely did not come from me. When he was young, he asked me to draw a cat or some other animal during church. I drew what he asked and he whispered, "That's not a cat!" So, I gave him the paper and pencil, and he drew an amazing drawing of the animal. This gift continued as he grew. Bruce and I thought the pictures he showed us of baseball players were traced until we saw him make excellent copies of the baseball cards he had been given.

Since Matt was smaller than some others, he was determined to prove his strength. His endurance and attitude gave him the initiative to start working at Hy-Vee when he was only fourteen years old. He also utilized his persuasive skills when he participated in mock trials in high school. Through this, he learned many skills that helped him later in life. He has always been a hard worker and very dependable.

In high school, he gave us a number of adventures. One of the most memorable was when he had knee surgery. They used a spinal block for his anesthesia. Matt woke up with a horrific headache from spinal fluid leaking. The doctors gave him a caffeine IV, which kept him wide awake all night. That really did not solve the problem, so the next step was a patch where the fluid was leaking. For several hours, I waited patiently in the location the staff asked me to wait. Finally, I asked the attendant where Matt was. She made some phone calls and told me, "It seems that we have lost your son's location." I could not believe my ears—lost my son! Evidently, there was a mix-up in directions, and Matt and the doctor wondered where I was and why I wasn't coming to his room. That was quite an experience! It is fun to remember many of his antics.

Ryan always seemed like the innocent child. Recently, we learned of some of the escapades that took place, and we were totally clueless. Apparently, he and the neighbor boy climbed a tree that had branches over the street and dropped water balloons on passing motorists. And this is only one example of his calculating personality.

As Ryan grew, he was interested in sports. He combined school with sports and work at Hy-Vee. His senior year in football was one of my most memorable moments. It was the last game of the season, and he was named co-captain of the team. I watched with pride as he walked out onto the field that night. The picture is etched in my memory, but the actual photo hangs in his childhood room.

There was another time when I came home and found Ryan and his friend Jeff in the kitchen. For Spanish class, they had to make non-alcoholic sangria for a class meal. I left to get some groceries, and when I returned, Ryan met me at the door. He had almost a fearful look on his face. As I walked in, I understood why. When the boys made the sangria, they added soda to the blender and neglected to replace the top. As they started the blender, sangria (purple fluid) flew all over the kitchen. It was on the ceiling, the cupboards, the appliances, and the floor.

I looked and then turned toward the door. I replied, "I'll be back when you get this cleaned up." They really did a pretty good job, but for a long time, we still found purple reminders in places we could not have imagined it would go.

Kari was always called Daddy's little princess when she was young. When she was totally disobedient one day, time outs and removing toys did nothing to change her behavior. Finally, I said, "That is it. You are getting a spanking!"

She looked at me with her hands on her hips and replied, "You can't spank me cuz I'm Daddy's little princess."

I replied, "Watch me." When Bruce came home from work, I told him what happened. He lovingly took Kari in his lap and explained that she would always be Daddy's little princess but Mommy was *queen bee*.

Each of our children are blessings from God. They have grown to be talented, unique individuals. God gifted them with different creative abilities they continue to use throughout their lives. I am amazed to see things they have made, drawn, created, or written, and then it is special to see these gifts and talents passed down to our grandchildren. Their faith has sustained each of them during trying times, and once again, it reminds me of my grandmother's prayers and others who prayed through the generations. Our God is faithful, and we can trust Him.

When times were financially difficult, God provided in unexpected ways—an unexpected refund check arrived, someone sent a birthday gift, and so many other blessings appeared. I admit I was often fearful, but seeing God at work and trusting Him to provide for all our needs drew me closer to Him. I needed to trust my Heavenly Father and grow in that trust. He was always there, but I needed to reach out to Him first. Each time I did that, I released control and gave it to the Master. Giving up control is an issue I have struggled with all my life. I want my way. It is a battle I fight every day. But when I surrender my will to His, His way is the best. It does not mean that everything works out great, but it allows me to grow closer to becoming the person I was created to be

CHAPTER 6 THOUGHTS

What were some of the challenges you faced as a young adult?

_____

_____

_____

_____

If you have children, what were some of your experiences?

_____

_____

_____

_____

What did you learn from them?

_____

_____

_____

_____

What things do you wish you would have done differently?

_____

_____

_____

_____

What is the most humorous experience you had during those years?

_____

_____

_____

_____

What broken pieces in your life did you recognize in this chapter?

_____

_____

_____

_____

STEPS

Have I not commanded you? Be strong and courageous. Do not be afraid; do not be discouraged, for the Lord your God will be with you wherever you go.
—Joshua 1:9

One Saturday morning, I was on my way to church to practice organ for the Sunday morning services and stopped at a red light. When it turned green, I entered the intersection at the same time a pickup truck came out of nowhere and hit my van on the driver's side door and spun my vehicle around. I had my seatbelt fastened, but the impact still threw my body in several directions. Instantly, I felt a severe headache, which was followed by more as the days progressed. We later learned the driver was under the influence at eight o'clock in the morning.

That day began a new world for me of constant headaches and severe pain in my neck and back. We tried everything from surgeries to pain clinics and medication. Nothing seemed to help, and the doctors told me I would "just have to live with the pain." I believed I could fix things in my life, so it was very difficult to hear I could not fix myself.

This accident rendered me unable to return to teaching. I received monthly disability payments but believed I was basically worthless. Many people in my situation would have lost hope. At first, I did lose hope, but I realized my worth and hope were not in what I was physically able or unable to do. My forever hope is in Christ. He is my strength, so I knew I could make a choice to either believe the lie that I was worthless, or I could trust in my Lord to see me through whatever laid ahead.

It was a challenge to struggle with physical pain every day. I was determined to be able to go back to work. I learned new ways to cope with the pain and challenged myself with what I could accomplish in a day. I celebrated every accomplishment, big or small, which gave me hope and courage for the next step.

Some days were frustrating. I am not a patient person, so it was hard to wait for someone else to do tasks I usually did. I am ashamed and sad that I was often short with my children and husband, so I asked them for forgiveness. Despite my anger with God that He allowed this to happen, I learned the lesson that He has a plan, and I needed to accept that. Because I knew my God was trustworthy, I needed to humble myself and accept His plan was so much better than mine. It was a time I was able to learn and grow closer to my Father.

Through numerous surgeries, I was fearful of the anesthetic every time. I wondered if I would I wake up and see my family or if I would wake up in Heaven. But my trust in my Heavenly Father and my hope in Christ sustained and comforted me. For various reasons, I had thirty surgeries, and faith, trust, and hope provided me strength, endurance, and comfort. Again, we see broken pieces. Sometimes, our daily needs feel overwhelming, and things seem hopeless. It is in these times our loving Father wants us to place our fears and needs in His hands so that He can use them for His good and to make our lives more valuable because of them.

A dear friend was praying for my healing during this time, which I had not known. She consistently and confidently prayed for years. About five years ago, my headaches and much of the pain went away. I am certain God answered her and others. Why did God choose to heal me? I do not have an answer. I only know that it was part of His plan for my life. I do not know why God heals some and not others, but I do know He has a plan for each of our lives. Sometimes, the healing is in the form of relief from the emotional effects of our pain. He provides grace and strength for each and every situation if we go to Him with our hurts. His way is always perfect even when we cannot see it. He is there ready and waiting to walk through whatever we face each day if we will only ask.

CHAPTER 7 THOUGHTS

Has anything ever derailed the plans you have for your life? What happened?

_____

_____

_____

_____

How did you handle that change or disappointment?

_____

_____

_____

_____

What have you learned from that experience?

_____

_____

_____

_____

Are you able to see the pieces God is putting together from this experience?

_____

_____

_____

_____

DOOR

*For we know that in everything God works together for good
for those who are called according to his purposes.*
—Romans 8:28

The same accident that changed my life also changed my perspective on what God was asking me to do with my future. I started to search for a different type of employment to allow me to work with my limitations. Long before the accident, I spent a couple of years in the financial services field and knew that was not the direction I wanted to pursue. I was not comfortable in a selling environment.

But because of my experience, I was invited by a government entity to assist people with how to handle their personal finances. It sounded exciting because it combined my love of teaching with my strong interest in personal finances. As I grew up, my parents, especially Dad, took every opportunity to teach me the value of money and how to give, save, and then spend. In my teenage years, Dad and I sat together yearly as he explained how to do the family tax returns. At first, I pretended to understand and be interested because it was a way to spend time with Dad. But as the years went by, I was amazed at my father's knowledge and understanding. The position I was offered seemed a perfect fit.

As I began the job, I created documents based on knowledge I learned from my father and from studying authors on those subjects. There were many challenges from the beginning. I quickly learned I was privileged to learn about finances. Many did not learn about personal finances, and I was shocked most people I met never had a savings account. People had overdue bills and no clue how to manage their money.

From that very naive beginning, I formed what became my passion for the years to come. It excited me to help people learn to use money *as God and Grandma intended. (That phrase is one Dave Ramsey uses.)*

I encountered clients whose marriages were broken due to finances. It is common knowledge that financial problems are the leading cause of divorce in the first seven years of marriage. I deeply wanted to help these families learn about their finances and come together as couples and avoid divorce. I encountered a couple who believed their only solution was bankruptcy, but after negotiations with creditors, we created a plan and a budget that worked. Instead of despair, they left with hope. I learned patience through that because others did not grow up like I did. It was such a joy to see the light bulb come on as my clients began to understand the basic concepts of personal finance and implement them in their lives.

Another challenge arose over a client who was dying of cancer. Though I helped my clients with their finances, I also prayed over them in my private prayer life. Because I worked for a government entity, I could not share my faith unless the client asked questions about it. Fortunately, they asked on a number of occasions. However, the man dying of cancer never asked. Though I prayed for opportunities to talk with him, it never happened. On the night he passed away, I walked into our kitchen with tears and exhaustion and told my husband, "I can't do it this way anymore."

Bruce is an extremely supportive husband and he simply said, "Then start your own program." I was astonished. Me, start a program? How would I do that? I turned to my Heavenly Father, filled with questions. As Bruce and I prayed, it became more and more obvious this was what God wanted me to do.

Through endless research, tears of frustration, and seemingly endless forms, to my joy my non-profit ministry was born. It was a trial and error start because I was completely new to forming a business. God was there, and He led me each step of the way, even when I could not see it. He brought together amazing people to be on the Board of Directors, and He continues to provide the right people. Once again, He took my broken pieces and wove them together for His plan.

At first, I saw clients in my home, but we soon realized some of the clients probably were not the best influences to be around our two youngest children, who were still not school age.

At that time, my friend was the local library director, and she offered me the opportunity to use one of the study rooms at the library to meet with clients. It was a wonderful set up because it was a place of anonymity for the client, and it gave me a workspace. The two biggest struggles with the arrangement were the amounts of material I had to carry with me and the problem of printing out items for clients.

After a period of time, a church in Sioux Center offered me offices in their building, and then a few years later, another non-profit in town allowed me to share offices with them. God's hands were in each of these moves. He led, and by His grace, I followed. All these blessings were amazing. I had a place to call home, and when I left my files in a locked file cabinet, I knew they were secure.

The ministry grew. A lady from Le Mars, Iowa, a town about twenty miles from Sioux Center, learned of the ministry and asked me to teach and assist people there with the same struggles. Suddenly, I had two offices, but I was not able to do the job alone because the work load was too large. Two very special people joined the ministry—what a blessing. I am truly thankful for each person God brought to the staff of this ministry. The Board was excited at the growth taking place and their support, encouragement, prayers, and love were vital to the growing mission—teaching people to use their money God's way.

Our Board of Directors expanded, and the guidance and direction they provided were invaluable. We learned together to listen to what God was preparing us for and where He was leading.

Some years later, several board members, staff, and volunteers remodeled a building, and since we had outgrown our facilities, we moved in to new offices. In the beginning, I could not have imagined the growth of this ministry. God's plans are always so much bigger than we can imagine, and when we trust Him and His leading, they come to fruition. These offices were truly a blessing from God. All along, He provided just enough for us to pay the bills each month. Many times, I doubted we would make our budget, but God came through every time. It was very obvious that this was His ministry, and He was providing our every need.

Once again, we needed larger offices as we grew. We had offices in five separate locations and were assisting a much larger numbers of clients. In addition, we offered classes for people to help them understand and grow in their understanding of their finances.

After eighteen years of heading this ministry, which was a blessing to me, I felt God wanted me to step down. I was truly tired. The stress of running a non-profit and the time it consumed took me away from so many things in my family life. We had grandchildren, and I wanted to be an integral part of their lives. At that time, little did I know what He had in store for me.

It was difficult to leave the ministry I began, but I knew one of God's plans was for me to assist start-up organizations. I received a call from La Salle University, located in Philadelphia, Pennsylvania, to discuss non-profit startups. To this day, I am not sure where they got my name, but God knows. As we talked, they asked if I would consider writing a book to help others begin their nonprofit journey. I kind of laughed because writing a book was never on my radar.

After thinking, praying, and seeking counsel from people I trusted, I began to write a book on non-profits. Honestly, I struggled with this. I believed God wanted me to do this, but I felt restless and uncomfortable with the project.

In October of 2018, we received word of the death of a young family friend we cared about very much. It was a very sad situation, and we mourned her loss. I saw the image of her face from a recent photo as I closed my eyes and slept that night. It was like God was using her to show me something. I felt like I was wrestling with God. *Lord, what do you want me to do? What are you trying to tell me?* The questions penetrated my heart all through that night until finally, I felt He wanted me to write this book. Again, I questioned God. *Who would want to read my story?* Suddenly, the answer was crystal clear, "If it changes one life, it is worth it." Wow! Who was I to argue with God?

I shared the dream with my husband the next morning. His laughing response was, "Do you need to be hit over the head with a two by four? Write the book!" Sometimes, I guess I am hard-headed, and it takes a sharp nudge to point me where God leads.

About this time, I was introduced to life coach, Niccie Kliegl, who lived in a neighboring town. She had written a book, and there was a study to accompany it. We started going through her book together, and almost immediately, she said she did not really know why we were doing this as a study because I really should be a life coach. As I looked back over the twenty plus years I spent financial coaching, I realized I had essentially been life coaching as well without realizing it. Niccie helped me start Hope Consulting Academy and has been a friend and mentor ever since.

My journey continues as I seek where God leads me with this book, but I know He has a perfect plan I can trust. Jeremiah 29:11, *"For I know the plans I have for you,"* declares *the Lord, "Plans to prosper you and not to harm you, plans to give you hope and a Future."*

CHAPTER 8 THOUGHTS

Have you ever made a decision that seemed strange or unusual to you, but you knew it was God's leading? If so, what was it?

_____

_____

_____

_____

Have you taken any *wrong turns* in your life? If so, what have you learned from that experience? How has it helped you grow?

_____

_____

_____

_____

What makes it difficult for you to know whether something is in God's plan for you?

_____

_____

_____

_____

Why is it so hard to step out in faith?

_____

_____

_____

_____

What pieces are you willing to give to God so He can make them into a thing of beauty?

_____

_____

_____

_____

MORTISE AND TENON

Do not be anxious about anything, but in every situation, by
prayer and petition, with thanksgiving,
present your requests to God.
—Philippians 4:6

Our family experienced another extremely difficult situation when our oldest daughter left home and for about two years, we did not know where she was. We did not know if she was dead or alive. We fell to our knees everyday and prayed for our daughter's safety and return home.

When you have a child that is missing, it is not uncommon for even some your best friends to pull away because no one knows how to respond. Whereas when you have a child that is sick or injured, people know what to say and do.

Emotions ran rampant during these times. I was in total despair somedays. At times, I could hardly get out of bed, and sometimes I was angry both at God and Chris. Somedays I had peace, but sometimes I was terrified. Each day brought different challenges.

I knew God was there, but it was difficult to read my Bible and pray because I was overwhelmed with emotions and doubtful Chris would be found.

One morning, I read my Bible at the kitchen table while drinking my morning coffee. The house was quiet because the other children had left for school. As I sat there, I felt extremely alone and did not know what to do. The tears that had been so plentiful were completely dry. I had no tears left to shed.

We believed our daughter was in the Sioux Falls area as she was attending college at a school there. We searched but did not receive assistance from the authorities She was close to one professor in particular, and she claimed to be a friend and helped Chris academically and in her life pursuits prior to this event. The professor lied to us repeatedly about Chris, as we learned much later. She had even moved Chris into her home without telling anyone, not even the college.

Finally, I began to pray, *Lord, I don't know if you are even still there. I am so alone and scared. What do I do? Lord, if someone would bring me some chocolate chip cookies, I would know you are there.* Afterward, I thought to myself, *Jan, that is the dumbest prayer you have ever prayed!* I am so grateful that God does not grade our prayers!

Later that morning, a friend of mine called. She asked if she could bring a casserole over for our evening meal. I remember looking at the phone and thinking, *It is not chocolate chip cookies, but it works for me!*

Later that morning, she brought over a box and set it on my kitchen counter. We talked, and she shared that she and her family were praying for us. That sentiment helped me to instantly know I was not alone. Tears of joy streamed down my face. I knew without a doubt that my Heavenly Father loved me.

After she left, I reached into the box to take out the casserole and put it in the refrigerator. As I lifted the dish out of the box, I realized there was something else underneath of it.

It was a plate of chocolate chip cookies! What a loving way He showed me how much he cared about the smallest details of my life, and that He would take care of our daughter. I can never look at a chocolate chip cookie the same way again!

Each one of us has a need for *chocolate chip cookies* in our lives. God knows the needs we have, and He is waiting to show us His love if we only ask. He cares about the tiniest details of our lives, and we need to open our eyes to see all the little things He does for us each day.

Again, I went through a crisis of belief. As I drove from Sioux Center to Orange City, I cried out to my Father. It was agony not knowing if Chris was okay or where she was. I pled with God to let me know how she was. At the corner where Highway 75 and Highway 10 intersect, I clearly heard the words, "Love her home."

"Love her?" I screamed. "I don't even like her!" I hollered. What a horrible response from a mother. I do not like even admitting that I said that. The stress of the situation had left me at that point, and I was overwhelmed with anger. Later, I bowed before God and begged for forgiveness, which He graciously gave.

But as I began to meditate on the words, *Love her home*, my heart began to change. It was a slow process, but I felt the love for my daughter blossom once again. It was a different kind of love—one of acceptance and love for my daughter. The broken pieces of both our lives were obvious, and God was working to make something better for both of us.

Several months later, I received a call from our daughter. She asked if she could come home. By that time, I honestly replied in a way I may not have a few months earlier, *Our door had always been open.* Just as in the story of the prodigal son, we welcomed her back to our family.

I wish I could tell you that everything worked out beautifully, but it did not. There were still some trials and struggles. But God used it to teach our family a great deal.

When Chris came home, I made a promise to myself that I would never ask her what had happened during the time she was gone or even why she was gone. If she chose to speak about it, then we would talk. I still operate under those conditions. When she opens up, I will listen. What she needed most was acceptance from me as her mom. I could reassure her that she was loved and cherished, and I would do anything I could to try to help her. When I look back, it is clear God was putting pieces back together in the best way, so much better than I would have imagined. It was He who allowed me to step back and listen. God provided that peace that only He can give, and I praise Him for it.

In Romans 8:28 we read, "*For we know that in everything God works together for good for those who are called according to his purposes.*" We so often miss that little preposition. It changes the meaning of the whole verse. That little word *in* means that God can take all the ugly, horrible things that happen in our lives and use them for good if we will only let Him. He takes the broken pieces of our lives and puts them back not just the way they were but into something so much better. His love for us is amazing!

CHAPTER 9 THOUGHTS

What are some difficult circumstances you have faced in your life?

_____

_____

_____

_____

How have those circumstances affected you?

_____

_____

_____

_____

Have those situations been resolved? If you are still in those situations, what can you change to bring resolution?

_____

_____

_____

_____

What part has God played in these circumstances?

_____

_____

_____

_____

Have your broken pieces been mended?

_____

_____

_____

_____

CRACKS

I am the way, the truth and the life. No one comes to the
Father but by me.
—John 14:6

On a beautiful Sunday afternoon in August, the shrill ring of the phone broke the peaceful silence. A weeping, crying, distraught voice on the line said, "Chad's been hurt. He was run over by a lawnmower." Chad is our grandson. Suddenly, I realized the voice was that of one of our daughter's close friends.

My heart stopped. I asked, "How is he?"

There was silence and then a shaking response, "Over half his foot is gone. The ambulance is on its way." Fortunately, Kari lived only a couple of blocks from the fire and EMT station in Sanborn. Sanborn was about eight miles from the hospital.

Immediately, Bruce and I called our other daughter, Chris. We picked her up from her house, and the three of us raced to the Sheldon Hospital where they had taken Chad. In my family, they call me *the lead foot,* so I drove. I knew I was well over the speed limit, but I looked at Bruce and said, "If you see red lights behind us, please call 911 and explain they can meet us at the hospital and give me any ticket they want." Fortunately, that was not necessary.

As we ran to the emergency department, we saw Chad's father, Andy, comforting the people involved in the accident. Bruce immediately went to our daughter, Kari, who was Chad's mother, as she cried hysterically. I walked to the stretcher where Chad was laying. He whimpered, and I could tell he was scared and uncomfortable. We learned that they could only give him a little pain medication for fear he would go into shock. He looked at me with big, teary eyes, and my heart felt like it had broken. From where I sat, his mangled foot was directly in my line of vision. That image is forever inscribed in my brain.

I stroked his head, talked softly to him, and prayed over him. His eyes looked at me with complete trust as if I could fix the situation. What a totally helpless feeling! But I knew the One who was already at work making something good come out of this terrible tragedy.

As soon as Kari calmed down, Bruce went to Chad. Ever since Chad was a tiny baby, Chad and Grandpa had a special bond. Whenever Chad was upset or couldn't calm down, Grandpa would sing "Jesus Loves Me," and Chad immediately relaxed. Many choruses of that song echoed through the emergency room that day. Finally, Kari came over. As she bent down to kiss Chad, he looked at her and said, "It's okay Mommy, don't cry. I"ll take care of you." He has such a sweet spirit. It seemed like we waited forever for the flight surgeon to arrive on the helicopter, but I am sure it was only a matter of minutes. It was coming from Sioux Falls, about seventy miles from where we were.

When the flight surgeon arrived, he looked at me and explained that because of the seriousness of the injury and the amount of equipment needed, no one could go with Chad in the helicopter. He asked if there was anything that could comfort him on the trip. I looked at him and said, "The only thing that calms him is singing 'Jesus Love Me.'"

The flight surgeon winked at me and said. "I've got this one. I know all the verses!" Immediately, a peace settled over me. God was in control. He loved and cared for Chad more than any of us could and had already provided comfort for him.

I could not watch the helicopter take off. It was one of the most helpless feelings of my life. Since I have *the lead foot* in the family, I drove Kari and Andy to Sioux Falls, along with Bruce and Chris. Chad's other grandparents also were on their way. We knew that surgery would have already begun by the time we arrived. I admit I definitely broke the law again getting to Sioux Falls, but if any patrolman tried to stop me, I would call, explain the situation, and tell them to please meet me at the Sanford Castle, which is the name of the children's hospital there and give me any citation they wanted. Fortunately, again that was not necessary.

We arrived in Sioux Falls and immediately learned that the best pediatric orthopedic surgeon in the region *just happened to be on call that weekend.* Coincidence? Absolutely not! It was a God Incidence!

The surgeon was miraculously able to save the tendon that later kept Chad's foot from dropping. As he saw other doctors at the Shriner's Hospital, they could not explain from the x-rays how that had even been possible. But we knew—God was working.

The incidents that most left an impression on my heart were when a doctor or nurse came into Chad's room and asked, "Chad, may I listen to your heart?" Chad always pointed to his chest and asked, "You mean here, where Jesus lives?" We will never know how many lives that little boy touched. Just thinking about it makes my eyes fill with tears as I see God's hand and His grace in the midst of such a dark situation.

We never know what the next day or even hour may bring. But we know without a doubt, He will be there with us each step of the way. Isaiah 22:6 says, " ...*a little child shall lead them.*" That was definitely the reality in this situation.

Today, Chad makes trips to the Shriner's Hospital in Minneapolis, about two hundred miles away, every three to six months depending on his rate of growth. He has adapted beautifully to his new normal. When asked to show the doctor his foot, he looks up and says, "Do you want to see my regular foot or my *awesome* foot?"

He runs, climbs, and swims because this is his new normal. Many people who look at him do not even realize he wears a brace. He plays with his friends, and they do not comment on his brace or his *awesome* foot. God has equipped children with amazing skills in adaptability. He relates to other children at Shriner's in such a sweet way. It is fun to watch the interaction as he sees many other children with more severe amputations. Their conversations are typical kid-type discussions. They do not see the differences that the world sees. That is truly a blessing.

When Chad started kindergarten, he absolutely loved school, especially the bus ride. On a ride home, another youngster came up and punched Chad in the mouth. Chad looked at him and said, "Thank you!" (The boy had knocked out Chad's loose tooth.) When my daughter told me about it, I immediately told her to call the school. I knew the next child the kid punched probably would not have the same reaction. When she called the school, she was glad she did because she learned this child had caused other problems. We asked Chad why he responded that way. His response was, "Now the tooth fairy will come!" We are thankful he took that approach.

For first grade, he entered a different school district. The move was very good for him as the teachers, students, and staff surrounded him with help, love, and acceptance. He feels accepted by the other students and is learning academics and how to be a friend.

Unfortunately, the amputation was not the only situation this little guy had to face. He also has dealt with severe asthma since he was tiny. Because of the massive doses of prednisone to help him breathe, he also developed cataracts. Those things were a lot for Chad and his family.

When Chad's accident happened, their house also had several inches of water in the basement due to torrential rains. The rain also destroyed their family room and many of the children's toys. Unfortunately, there were three times in one summer a few years later that intense rain caused flooding and a high water table, so there was no other place for the water to go. The family faced illnesses, medical expenses, and disappointments, but the family is such a blessing as they continue to live in faith knowing God has a plan for each one of them.

In the midst of this turmoil, their family was blessed with a precious little girl they named Karli Josephine after Kari's maternal grandmother. Karli is a bundle of energy, mischief, and love all in one. Papa is her favorite, but Grandma is fine if Papa isn't available.

We count our blessings daily that their faith has sustained them through these trials. We all know God has a purpose and will take all of these things and make something beautiful out of them as only He can do.

Their lives can be pretty much summed up in Chad's favorite songs, "Our God is an Awesome God," and "Raise a Hallelujah."

CHAPTER 10 THOUGHTS

What challenges are you currently facing?

_____

_____

_____

_____

Are there disappointments in your life so deep you feel unable to talk about them? If so, you can write them down here. God knows, and He wants you to come to him with them.

_____

_____

_____

_____

Are there any special scripture verses that bring you comfort?

_____

_____

_____

_____

What pieces of your life can you see God putting back together today?

_____

_____

_____

_____

RENOVATION

The Lord is my strength and my shield, in Him my heart trusts, and I am helped; my heart exalts, and with my song I give thanks to Him.
—Psalm 28:7

More recently, there were unexpected adventures. After a routine exam by my doctor, I received a call I had to return to the clinic for a scan, and we awaited the results.

Our medical provider posts results on the online portal as soon as they are available. When I was alone, I read them. I read that I had a spot on my right kidney that looked like a *textbook* case of kidney cancer. The doctor suggested I have it removed as soon as possible. As I sat there alone, I felt an amazing peace come over me. I knew in the inmost part of my being that all would be okay, no matter what came.

A few days later, we walked into the doctor's office. He came in the room, looked at the chart, flipped through pages, and cleared his voice. He was obviously very uncomfortable. Before he could speak, I looked at him and said, "I read the report online."

He looked at me in amazement. He said, "And you are sitting there as calmly as can be."

I replied, "I know the news, and whatever happens is in God's hands."

I went into surgery not knowing what the outcome would be but I knew whose hands held the outcome. After surgery, the doctor said he had removed a small portion of my right kidney along with the tumor, which would be tested. Several days later, I received a call from the doctor who said, "I am very rarely wrong in my diagnosis, but I am so happy I was wrong with yours. The tumor was completely benign." Immediately, I thanked my Father for this news as tears ran down my face. I wondered why I was blessed with this outcome when so many others do not receive that news. I may not have the answer, but I know that my Heavenly Father has a plan, and He is working it out in my life. We rejoiced as a family and realized God put pieces together in His special way, yet again.

Soon after that experience, I received a phone call while at work. "This is DHS, and you need to pick up your grandson Chad in Sheldon in a half hour." Sheldon is a town about 35 minutes from my office. I explained I was with a client and needed to finish the appointment, but the voice was stern. "You need to pick him up, *now*." When I asked what was going on. I learned our daughter and her two children were being removed from their home because of a domestic violence issue in their family. Chad told DHS the only place he felt safe was at our home, and could he come to our house? Of course, they could! I was completely shocked at this news, because we did not know what had been taking place in our daughter's home. Over the next weeks, we learned some shocking details that broke our hearts. I really cannot go into the details at this time, but it was an unhealthy situation for our daughter and her two children.

By about 7:30 that evening, our daughter and grandchildren were settled in our home. It was a tight squeeze because our home is not that large, but we were happy they were safe.

For the next few months, we navigated the Department of Human Services system with all its quirks and rules that did not always make sense. We understood the rules are set up for reasons, but at times, it appeared the person who caused the issue was more protected than the helpless children in the situation. The times in court were very difficult, and Kari was torn apart by what had taken place. She and the children needed to heal, and that was an ongoing process. Chad enrolled in our local school system and immediately did better in school. The staff surrounded him with comfort and love, and the children welcomed him into their classroom and their lives. It was truly a blessing to see him thrive in school and to know that others cared deeply for him.

Those months were not easy. It was hard for all of us to adjust to being in a home together. Two empty nesters suddenly had a two-year-old and a six-year-old twenty-four hours a day, seven days a week. It was a huge change.

Truthfully, it did not always run smoothly, but there were laughter and tears. It is never good to see a broken family, and the wounds run deep. Healing takes a great deal of work and time. As a parent, it is heartbreaking to watch your child and grandchildren in that experience. Parents want the best for their children, so knowing they are in pain is hard.

I do not think anyone ever expects to experience that type of situations in their life. We definitely were not prepared for it. Home had a different meaning than it did before they moved in. I realized I was not as patient as I needed to be. God continues to work on this area of my life. Also, I liked order and things in their *proper* place in my home. In a home with young children, that does not happen. It requires adjustments. But I realized that my adjustments and Bruce's were small compared to the ones our daughter and grandchildren faced.

There were blessings amidst the adjustments also. Chad decided he wanted to be baptized. He wanted it so badly. He literally dragged me to the front of the church to talk to our pastor. Chad was dedicated as a baby, but this is not a discussion as to how infants should be brought to Jesus. In his heart, He knew he wanted to be baptized because He loves Jesus. That is an answer to prayers over the generations. At the time of writing this book, a good friend is mentoring Chad to make an age-appropriate profession of faith at the same time he and Karli are baptized. Again, God is mending lives, putting pieces back together in a beautiful way.

Also, Chad was chosen by Team Impact to partner with a college sports team. His team is the Northwestern College Red Raiders baseball team. What an opportunity for him to spend quality time with these godly young men. We had the privilege of meeting the coach and some of the players. We were impressed with their dedication to this program, their outpouring of love and acceptance for Chad, and their hearts for Jesus.

For me, someone who wants to fix things, I cannot fix my situation. The pain and anguish that situations like this cause is almost indescribable. Thankfully, our Heavenly Father knows and understands. He loves all of us equally because we are His children. His love never changes. He never changes. His promises are as true today as they were back in the Old Testament. He is the same yesterday, today, and forever.

These situations are not about who is right and who is wrong. They are about healing and restoration. Some relationships are unrestorable, but God is in that decision as well. Often, we tend to form opinions about what people should or should not do. That is not what we are called to do. We are called to love even the unlovable. We are to be like Christ to those who are hurting and need His healing touch. Each situation is unique and must be met with understanding and acceptance from all the people involved.

It is a privilege to live with these grandchildren and hopefully teach them values, especially to be able to trust again. Their little hearts were broken. They cannot understand what happened in their world and lives and why things changed.

At the first hearing, I sent a message to their dad through his lawyer. I asked her to tell him that we still loved him. She blinked and said she had never been asked to do that before. I explained that love is a choice, and Bruce and I chose to love, but not because we are such great people, but because we love a God who sent His son to die for us. If He can do that for us and for all the sins we have committed, then we are called to choose love in places like this.

I would really encourage anyone going through this experience to reach out in love. It changes your perspective and helps remove anger. It changes fear into trust. This is truly what each of us is called to do, and it does make a difference.

Life will never be the same again. Does that mean we give up? No, it means we diligently seek God's will and His purpose in all that is taking place. We need to turn to Him first before we make decisions. He must be our anchor in the storm.

CHAPTER 11 THOUGHTS

What unexpected events are you facing?

_____

_____

_____

_____

How have you chosen to handle these events?

_____

_____

_____

_____

What are some of the hard decisions you have had to make?

_____

_____

_____

_____

What pieces are being put together right now in your life by forgiving?

_____

_____

_____

_____

HOME

By this time, I am sure many of you are wondering about the titles of the chapters of this book. Please take a moment to reflect on them. As you do, I hope you will see that they are architectural terms used to build a house. During those chapters, we were talking about building not a house, but a *home*.

Home. That word brings all kinds of thoughts and memories to mind. Our home is a place where we live, work together, argue, disappoint, encourage, love, and so much more. It is where we experience life.

This year especially, the word *home* has more meaning. We recently lost my mother-in-law at age ninety-three. We were blessed to have her with us for many years, but she was the last of our parents to leave us for their heavenly home. The word *home* brings sadness for those no longer with us. But it brings joy for the privilege of being with the next generations as we celebrate the birth of Christ. It brings excitement as we anticipate what the little ones will accomplish in their lives, and it brings hope that one day, we will all be together again.

Really, our home is not an actual place, but it is the people who are in our lives that mean so much to us. As we look at the pieces God has already put together in such a more beautiful and valuable way, we are blessed.

Maybe you are wondering where our children have gone. Each has taken a different path because of their unique gifts. We are so pleased to see what God has done in each of their lives.

Chris graduated from Iowa State University with the idea of going into teaching. This plan was derailed when our local library was destroyed by arson. She worked there in the summer, so she chose to remain and assist the director in getting a library up and running from the ruins. She is very creative and very skilled with tools. Once again, that did not come from my genes. We love the way she cares for and loves on all the nieces and nephews who have joined our family.

Our oldest son, Matt, is doing very well. He graduated from Iowa State University with a degree in landscape design. His designs amaze me. Many designs in Central Iowa have been created by him. His creative ability definitely did not come from me. His knowledge of horticulture and his ability to select just the right plants and materials are great and I truly believe those interests came from both of his grandmothers.

After his first year of college, Matt married the love of his life, Colleen. Later, they were blessed with twin boys, Trey and Jake. The boys were born on my birthday, September 11th. This was truly the best birthday gift ever! Even though they were very small, both grandmas were able to be in the NICU and give the boys their bottles. Children are so special, but grandchildren are even more delightful. It hit me. I was a grandma. Wow. There is no better feeling than that.

We have been blessed to watch these boys grow up, act in a number of plays, and perform amazing musical concerts. It has been such a joy to watch them grow into young men. It is hard to believe they are in their first year of college.

Then, two years ago, Matt and Colleen were blessed with a little girl they named Renley. It is such fun to see the boys wrapped around their little sister's finger. She is a sweetheart and so much fun to be around.

Ryan, our second son, learned a great deal from his older brother, especially the concept of hard work and ethics. He was involved in sports, school and friends while working at our local Hy-Vee. He very much enjoyed English and writing. Ryan went on to college at Northwestern College in Orange City and received a degree in Business. Right after graduation, he moved to Des Moines to work for a large corporation there. He has proved his abilities and skills over the years. While working on his Master's Degree, he met a wonderful girl named Stacy, who stole his heart. Their wedding was beautiful, and several years later, they welcomed Halle into their lives. She was born on Ryan's birthday—do we see a pattern here? Halle is a little charmer, and we wish we could spend more time with her. When we stay with them, Ryan always tells Halle jokingly that the *basement trolls* have come to visit. She loves that. She frequently asks Mom and Dad in the morning if the basement trolls came because she is usually asleep when we get to their home.

Kari and her children continue to live with us. Every morning I am greeted with "Morning, Grandma. Coffee?" Karli and I have a special routine that reminds me of my childhood. Coffee with Grandma continues.

Chad does not allow his injury to affect his life. He fearlessly climbs trees, runs (often without his prosthesis), and does typical boy activities. Right now, Kari's social work degree is on hold as she is needed and loved as a full-time mom. In the meantime, she completed her EMT training and has really enjoyed being part of a squad.

As you can see, we have a special family. We are blessed by each one who has joined our lives, and we are grateful to God for His blessings. Once again, we see the broken pieces of thinking we would never have children, which God wove into something much more valuable and beautiful than we could have ever imagined.

This is truly our home! God took our house and changed it into a home. For this, we are extremely grateful. It is built on the foundation of our confidence in God and His work in our lives uniting us as a family. Our hearts are filled with memories of good times and difficult ones, but the overarching theme is: *In everything, God has worked together for good.* We will never see the grand picture this side of heaven, but He has always been with us.

My prayer is that you will be blessed by sharing our home with us and by the chapters that follow, which define so much of my life. May you see the pieces of your life being put back together by the touch of the Master's hand.

CHAPTER 12 THOUGHTS

Is your place of residence, a house, or a home?

_____

_____

_____

_____

Why did you answer the way you did?

_____

_____

_____

_____

Are there any changes you would like to make in your house or home? If so, what would they be?

_____

_____

_____

_____

What pieces of your life are being changed in your home?

_____

_____

_____

_____

FORGIVENESS

*"Bear with each other and forgive one another if any of you has
a grievance against someone. Forgive as the Lord forgave you.*
—Colossians 3:13

Several years ago, I had to face the issues I had been running
from for much of my life. The first issue of abuse from my
childhood had affected my life in so many ways. It made me
fearful, very wary, and untrusting. I had kept my promise for
much of my life until I finally told my husband.

He was so loving and kind. He did not view me as damaged
goods. He loved me just because of who I was. He encouraged
me to forgive. How could I forgive someone who had hurt
me in so many ways? By that time, the person who had hurt
me was dead. Why did it matter?

I began to study forgiveness. As I let God speak to me
through His Word, I realized how much He had forgiven me.
He had given His only son to die a bitter, painful, shameful
death on a cross for all the things I had done wrong, called
sin. Jesus freely and willingly gave His life for me. He did not
have to do that, but He did. He obeyed His Father. Before

Jesus came to earth, perfect animals were sacrificed to pay for the sins of the people. Jesus came to earth as a baby from the perfection of Heaven and being with the Father to live in our world. He did so because of His love for us. The only way for our sins to be forgiven is by a sacrifice. This was God's redemption plan for His people. Every last drop of Jesus' blood was shed on the cross to pay for each of our sins. He loves us that much!

As these truths began to sink into the deepest part of me, I realized I needed to forgive as Jesus has. Forgiveness was for *me*. It did nothing to the person who hurt me. It was to change me and take away the bitterness, shame, guilt, and hurt that filled my heart and replace it with God's love, peace, and joy.

Part of the healing process was learning to believe I was no longer damaged goods. This was definitely the hardest part. It required a total change of mindset. Believing in yourself after being traumatized is very hard. With God's Word and His help, I started to see how important and valuable I was to my loving, heavenly Father. In His Word, he repeatedly says how much He loves us. In Psalm 8:4-5, the psalmist asks the question, *"What is man that You are mindful of him . . . You have made him a little lower than the angels."* Psalm 36:7 tells us, *"How precious is your steadfast love, O God!"* God's love for us is immeasurable. When I began to accept that I was loved just as I was by the Creator of the universe, the one who had made me in His image, my heart began to change. I was really worthy of being loved and loving others. Before, I believed the deep ache, unworthiness, and ugliness was not replaced by His love, joy, and peace. At times, the questions of my worth still attempt to conquer me, but as Romans 8:37 says, *"No, in all these things we are more than conquerors through Him who loved us."* I will probably continue to fight this battle, but each time it happens, the struggle is easier because deep down, I am convinced that my Father's love is unfailing.

By not forgiving, the only person we hurt is ourselves. Without forgiveness, our hearts harden. We cannot truly come close to our Father.

We often mistakenly think that forgiving someone *lets them off the hook*. That is not what forgiveness is. They still committed the wrong, and forgiveness does not make it right. That person will need to answer for their actions, but it is not up to us to be the judge and jury.

Instead, forgiveness releases us to be the person God designed us to be. It frees us to know Him more clearly, to see Him for who He truly is, the Lord of the universe. It helps us to realize that the Creator is so in love with us that He was willing to make a way for us to be reunited with Him. And He was willing to sacrifice His son to do so.

I cannot imagine giving one of my children up to die for someone else, but that is exactly what God did when He sent Jesus into this world. His love is beyond comprehension, and His grace is amazing!

Forgiveness is costly. It costs us the right for revenge. It may cost us in other ways, too, possibly even financially. But think of the cost God paid for each one of us. Jesus willingly gave His life so that we could have life. Giving a life is the greatest gift anyone can offer. That is what God allowed Jesus to do because of His tremendous love for each of us. His desire is that we all come to Him as one of His children. He does not want to lose anyone. The reality is that many will not understand or accept this free gift. In John 14:6, it tells us, *"I am the way and the truth and the life. No one comes to the Father except through me."* Jesus is the answer.

Forgiveness is also a path to restoration with the one who has caused us pain. True forgiveness recognizes the gift we have been given by God and allows us to give that gift to the one who injured us. The greatest result of forgiveness, besides our restoration with our Heavenly Father, is the ability to restore the relationship we previously had with the one who hurt us. Now, this is not always practical or possible, but when it can happen, there is such an indescribable sweet release and healing.

Take a good look at the word forgiveness. What is in the center? Suddenly you will see the word "give". When we forgive, we give our anger, hurts, and our disappoints to God. They are then in His hands. We no longer own them because we have given them to the One who loves us completely. The gifts we receive from the Father are so much more valuable. He gives us peace and joy that we could otherwise not experience.

Recently at our church, we had a special service of forgiveness and healing. Each of us received a special piece of paper and a pen. We had the opportunity to write down our sins, confess them to our Father, and then either put them in a bowl of water or hand them to an Elder and ask that person to pray for us. Then, they put the paper into the water. The paper dissolved as they stirred the water. This was such a great illustration and image of what happens when we confess our sins. Not only are we forgiven, but our sin is washed away by the blood of our Savior, Jesus Christ. Our sins are gone! Christ's blood has covered them, and even though we still remember them, God has washed us clean, and He remembers them no more. Wow. We are clean, white as snow. What an amazing feeling to watch that paper disappear. How can we not come to our Father and ask for forgiveness when the results bring such peace and healing? We are whole again, washed by the blood of the Lamb.

Forgiveness is possible. It is a gift from our Father, and it is a gift that can be shared in certain circumstances. God is always ready and waiting with open arms to forgive and restore us. His love is greater than we can ever comprehend, and He wants that relationship with us, His children. He is the author and the protector of our faith. He is the great I Am!

CHAPTER 13 THOUGHTS

What does forgiveness mean to you?

_____

_____

_____

_____

Why do you think forgiveness seems so hard?

_____

_____

_____

_____

Who specifically are you struggling to forgive?

_____

_____

_____

_____

How is not forgiving hurting you?

_____

_____

_____

_____

What pieces do you see God putting back together in your life?

_____

_____

_____

_____

GRACE

As a young child, I learned GRACE was God's Riches At Christ's Expense. That is a great thought, but we really need to have a more concrete understanding of grace. It is truly the unmerited favor of God. It means that God is not giving us what we deserve. If we look at our lives, we can point to many *good* things we have done. But why have we accomplished them and for what reason? If we are honest with ourselves, most of our motives have been somewhat selfish. That is part of being human. Yes, we have helped the poor, supported a missionary, maybe even went on a mission trip, and the list continues.

When we really contemplate our lives, at least part of what we have done for others has really helped make us feel good too. There is nothing wrong with any of these things in themselves, but we need to really think about grace.

What can we really do to make ourselves right with God? Nothing. God loves us so much that He provided a solution in the form of the gift of His Son to pay the ultimate price for our sins. Imagine—giving His son to pay for our sins. What love is this? A love greater than *all* the sins of the world. Our Father is perfect and completely without sin. We cannot be in His presence unless we are covered with the blood of Jesus because of His perfection.

Grace is truly not giving us what we really deserve. None of us can say that we have never done anything wrong or hurt someone else either on purpose or without really knowing it.

We tend to rate some sins as worse than others. In reality, there is no difference. Sin is sin! It separates us from God because He is without sin. Sin does not come in different degrees or sizes. It is sin, and there is only one solution—Jesus Christ.

God's love for us is so great that we cannot even comprehend it. "Grace that Is Greater than All Our Sins" is a song with such meaningful words. It speaks about how great God's grace truly is, so much greater than our sins. It is all because of Christ's death and resurrection. The words to the song "Your Grace Still Amazes Me," touched my life so much I chose it for my dad's funeral. I am amazed each day that God continues to love me through all my failures and fears. He will never leave me or forsake me. What amazing grace and love we are offered.

How can a perfect, all-knowing, ever-present God love a sinful creature like me? I have no answer except that His love is greater than anything I have ever done or will do. His grace is totally undeserved. His grace is totally beyond human comprehension.

The Lord of the universe loves you and me so much that He wants a relationship with each of us. But He has given us the ability to make choices because He does not want us to be puppets on a string. He loves us so much that He wants us to *choose* Him. When we make poor choices, God mourns those choices, but He continually draws us back to Him because of His amazing grace and love.

This choice is His gift to us. Oh, how He desperately wants you to choose Him. His desire is that all will know and accept His saving grace. The best part is that it is free. Yes! Free!

All we have to do is to say *yes* to His invitation. That yes will change your life forever. He is always reaching for you, drawing you to Himself, loving you no matter what you have done.

There is nothing you can do to make God love you more, and there is nothing you can do to make Him love you less. Once you understand this basic idea, it is easier to say yes to His amazing grace and unending love. Choose God's invitation today. Saying yes is one of the hardest things you will ever do and yet one of the easiest. It is hard because it means you must surrender control of your life to the One who loves you most. It is easy because all you need to do is ask. Simply reach out to God. He is waiting with open arms. Tell Him you need Him. He really already knows it, but He wants to hear it from you. Ask Him to forgive your sins because you know that Jesus died for you. Ask Him to come and live in your heart and be the Lord of your life. He is waiting. Run to His open arms.

CHAPTER 14 THOUGHTS

What does Grace mean to you?

_____

_____

_____

_____

How have you recently shown grace to someone?

_____

_____

_____

_____

Is it hard to accept God's grace? If so, why do you believe you have a problem accepting it?

_____

_____

_____

_____

What are some examples in your life where you have experienced God's grace?

_____

_____

_____

_____

HOPE

What is hope? In Philippians 1:6, it tells us *"Being confident of this, that He who began a good work in you will carry it on to completion until the day of Christ Jesus."* Those words give us hope, but what is it really? Hope is trust in what we cannot see and are not yet experiencing. It is believing that the promises God has given us are true. It is trusting that Jesus Christ really did come to earth, lived among us, died on the cross, and rose again because He loved us.

Hope is very difficult for those in hard places. We can know in our heads that God is there and that He knows the plans He has for us, but finding the link from our heads to our hearts can be hard.

People in traumatic situations, disasters, and loss usually lose hope quickly. This is not unusual. Self-worth and hope are closely tied together. Statistics show that when disasters strike and people lose their homes, the suicide rate rises dramatically. When life seems hopeless and without a purpose, many people have nowhere to turn. Maybe the situation you are in seems hopeless. Maybe your finances are in a mess, and you can see no way out. Maybe your marriage is in shambles, and you feel that no one loves you.

To tell you to have hope at this time would be a disservice to you. The loss is real. It is okay to mourn that loss and work through the grief. You may not be able to do this alone, and that is okay. There are trained people who can help you. Most of all, reach out to your Father. He loves you just as you are, and His arms are open wide to welcome you back into His fold.

A favorite verse of mine is Isaiah 40:31. *"But those who hope in the Lord will renew their strength. They will soar on wings like eagles; they will run and not grow weary, they will walk and not be faint."* These words provide comfort that even in the darkest hours. God is still there. He cares. He wants us to run to Him for comfort, and He will provide strength. That does not mean that our problems will disappear. They may even increase. But no matter what happens, God is there. He is with us and cares for us because we are His children. Nothing can separate those who have accepted Jesus as Savior from Him. Even though the earth shakes and our faith wavers and people turn their backs on us—Jesus never will.

Hope is a quantity that we cannot see or measure. It is not just a feeling, but it is more than that. It is a belief and trust in what is not seen. We have not seen God, but we have seen Him at work so many times that we often take Him for granted. Have you heard a baby's first cry? How about the leaves turning color in the fall? Have you not experienced that beauty? What about the waves splashing on a white sand beach? Who made this all and set the stars in space?

If our God can create the universe with a few words as we read in Genesis 1:16, *". . . And the stars also."* How can we not trust in Him to care for us as well? This is hope.

In Mark, it talks about having faith the size of a mustard seed, the smallest of all seeds on earth. God doesn't measure our faith by its size. He only asks us to trust Him, put our faith in Him, and He will do the rest. By trusting Him, we can have hope for the present and for the future.

During many dark times in my life, I leaned on those promises. When I was recovering from the abuse, a wise friend asked me, "Where was Jesus when all this was taking place?" As I pondered that question, I realized that during that time, Jesus was actually there with me. He was right beside me. He was crying and hurting with me—He was *there* with me. When I finally could run to Him, He covered me with His feathers, and He washed me clean because of His death on the cross for me. He began to heal my broken heart and spirit.

This did not happen overnight. It was a process. As we grow in our faith and knowledge of Christ, we realize that we need to run to Him right away when these things happen.

When Chad was hurt, my heart could actually praise God because He had provided not only the best orthopedic pediatric surgeon in the Midwest, but also a doctor who was a Christ follower. Wow! Even in the midst of tragedy, we can see God's hand at work. That is hope.

After we lost our first child, I do not really believe I took the time to grieve that loss, which is exactly what that was. It is not only the loss of a child but also the loss of a dream. I screamed at God. He knew I was angry already because He knows our words and thoughts even before they are in our minds. He did not give up on me because I was His child. Slowly, He began to take the broken pieces of my life and my dreams and plans, and began to put them back together into something that was His plan. It was something that was more beautiful and valuable than anything I could have ever imagined. He gives hope because *He is Hope*. He is not far away. He is right there waiting for you to come running to Him with all your failures, hurts, broken dreams, and disappointments. He is there to give you hope. That intangible word that changes lives. He is Hope.

CHAPTER 15 THOUGHTS

What does hope mean to you?

_____

_____

_____

_____

What things make you discouraged?

_____

_____

_____

_____

How does hope give you confidence for the future?

_____

_____

_____

_____

What is your hope built upon?

_____

_____

_____

_____

AFTERWORD

When we look at our lives and really examine what is important to us, we find that we constantly are looking for hope. We realize that our hope truly can only come from Jesus Christ and our relationship with Him. He sustains us. He loves us more than can ever imagine or comprehend. When we forgive, we draw closer to our Father's heart and experience. His grace still amazes us daily. This is my prayer for you as we have journeyed together.

Your Next Steps in learning about forgiveness:

- Complete the questions in the book

- Purchase the accompanying study guide of *Finding Value in a Cracked Pot, Joy in Forgiveness*

- Contact Jan for personal life coaching

  jan@hopeconsultingacademy.com

Financial Coaching

- Do you want to learn to use your resources God's way?

- Do you want to get out of and stay out of debt?

- Do you want financial freedom?

Contact Jan at:

jan@hopeconsultingacademy.com
to set up your personal coaching sessions

FINANCIAL

Consultants

- Learn how to stop hiding from your past
- Connect with God so that you can live the life He designed for you
- Get rid of the false labels you have believed
- Do you want to know *Your Secret Name?*

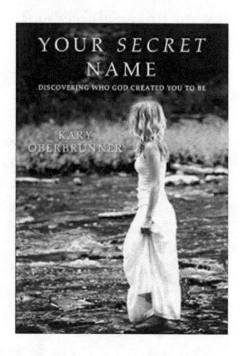

Jan is a certified coach and wants to help you to become the person God created you to be.

Contact:
jan.henryson@yoursecretname.com

- Find your purpose in life
- Learn who you are in Christ
- Learn to find peace, joy and love in your days

Jan is a certified
Awaking the Living Legacy Life Coach,
and would love to help you find meaning and purpose in
your life.

Contact:
jhenryson@gmail.com

Would you like Jan to speak to your church or group?

Please inquire about availability and pricing at:

jan@hopeconsultingacademy.com

Website: www.hopeconsultingacademy.com